Living Large
on Little

How to See the Invitation in Limitation

Anna Elkins

ISBN: 9781696266697

For the plum tree on Two-Mile Drive
in Kalispell, Montana

Table of Contents

Gratitude

Gratitude to WordSpaceStudios where I worked on this book during a writing residency. The studio is located in San Francisco, a city consistently rated as one of the most expensive in the country—a perfect place to practice living large on little.

Gratitude to my friends and family who have bought my books and art, given me inexpensive rent, asked me to write this book, and—most beautifully—given me the encouragement to keep being a poet and painter even when it didn't (or still doesn't) make financial sense.

And gratitude to grace—the only way this all works.

i

Without bitterest cold that penetrates to the very bone, how can plum blossoms send forth their fragrance all over the world?

—Matsuo Basho

Seeds

♦ ♦ ♦

It's one of the paradoxes of life and poetry: restriction invites creativity.

A girl born in poverty in Mississippi works her way to become the wealthiest woman in the world. A writer confines himself to metrics and writes dozens of plays in blank verse that continue to be performed centuries later.

We may never reach the level of Oprah or Shakespeare, but if we're willing, we can see our own limitations as invitations.

We can expand our imagination to see beyond obstacles.

We can live large on little.

◆◆◆

A few shoulds before I continue...

I should note that I have never had a trust fund or a wealthy husband (or an unwealthy husband for that matter). And as a freelancer, I have not had a consistent source of income for a over a decade. Even so, I've been able to live an abundant life and to work and travel on six continents, and people have often asked me how. This little book is my way of offering an answer.

I should also note that I live in the USA, a country whose poor are still richer than people in most of the world. I am aware of the complexities of class and culture and that regardless of how little money I might have, I am still writing this from a place of privilege—privilege of being raised in a loving home with both parents, of having an education, and of the many freedoms and gifts that previous generations made possible. I am thoroughly and consistently grateful for all of those things.

And I should note that I am a poet, not a banker, so this book isn't filled with straight-up tips for spending less, nor does it offer investment strategies.

This book *is* about spending less time seeing limitations as obstacles, and it *is* about investing in our imagination to re-see obstacles as invitations. In fact, you might say this book is about revision—*re*-vision.

Because much of life and writing is about seeing again.

And again.
And again.[1]

◆ ◆ ◆

In all honesty, I'm astonished that I've made it more than halfway through a natural lifespan as a poet and painter. Granted, a chunk of that lifespan was spent as a dependent in grade school. Still, in my pre-Internet childhood, I didn't know anyone who lived a freelance life— either on their own or with support. Any non-traditional life I read about in books seemed literally and figuratively bound to remain in pages.

◆◆◆

I grew up mostly in rural Montana. At the edge of our field grew a young plum tree. I loved this tree. I whispered my hopes to it and sat in its shade and...I was probably reenacting Shel Silverstein's *The Giving Tree*. I was a bit of a romantic.

Beneath that tree, I dreamed what my life would be like when I grew up. Though I can't remember all of those dreams, I do remember that my imagination sustained me.

The farmhouse my parents rented was beautiful and old—over a hundred years at the time. It had no central heating. In the winter, our pipes would consistently freeze. The spigot mounted to the fence leaked enough water to create fantastical, three-foot-high ice sculptures.

Winter mornings, my brother David and I would don our scarves, coats, hats, mittens, and Moon Boots and plunge through the snow to see what shape had grown in the night.

One year, the spigot dripped into being an ice chair worthy of the witch of Narnia. It was so big we could sit on it, and we did—taking turns being King and Queen, reigning over the white and gray landscape—ours to the edge of the visible world.

This world is but a canvas to our imagination.

—Henry David Thoreau

♦ ♦ ♦

The imagination is a mighty thing. Let's play with it for a moment.

Picture yourself on a sunny fall afternoon, standing beneath a big, leafy plum tree—its fruit purple and ripe. You reach up into the branches and pull down a perfect plum. Your fingers leave a sheen on the untouched skin.

When you bite into the fruit, the flavor is bright and sweet. Each and every plum on that tree represents many seasons of growth and tending.

What if we cultivated a green thumb of imagination? And what if our daily choices grew over the years to yield good, sweet fruit?

◆ ◆ ◆

On the brink of sleep, when many good ideas make it past the analytical gates of day, the thought came to me to organize *Living Large on Little* into nine sections based on ancient attributes: the fruit of the Spirit.

Strange, I know. But strangely, it worked.

Nine qualities comprise these fruit: love, joy, peace, patience, kindness, goodness, faithfulness, gentleness, and self-control.

And so....

I've written this little book in little sections for each of those qualities—leaving lots of white space for you to pause and dream and jot and sketch any ideas that might arise as you read.

In fact, as I was writing this book, I was sketching, too. I thought it would be fun to choose fruit to illustrate the nine sections. But which fruit? O, too many options! So, embracing limitation as helpful artistic strategy, I decided on tree fruit.[2] Mostly, the illustrated fruit are just hinted at in the sections, but their presence was a helpful touchstone while I wrote.

Here's to seeing the tree in the seed.

Here's to standing beneath the tree and remembering the seed.

That's living large on little.

---

[2] Dear plum tree on Two-Mile Drive: if you're still there, I hope those long Montana winters are helping your blossoms be fragrant and your fruit be sweet.

Great things are done by a series of small things brought together.
                              —Vincent Van Gogh

Love

◆◆◆

Pomegranates are often a symbol of love, which is partly why I chose them to illustrate this quality.

I also chose them because a man in a market in India once showed me how to open them. And then a woman in Spain showed me another way to open them. It makes a nice metaphor: the many ways we can open into love.

The pomegranate is packed with so many juicy, jewel-y seeds. There is nothing like breaking open a section and dripping the crimson juice down your fingers. It can be messy and marvelous, tart and delicious.

Like love.

And living large on little.

What you remember saves you.
—W. S. Merwin

◆◆◆

Our world may not agree on much, but if we were to agree on something, it would probably be that love is The Most Important Thing.

We want the best for the people we love—ourselves included. Problem is: we buy into fear-based marketing that tells us if we love ourselves, we'll buy ourselves a new car. If we love our partners, we'll buy them diamond-studded bling, and if we love our children, we'll buy them a trip to that Really Big Amusement Park.

Our world might also agree that love and money are not synonyms.

But it can be easy to forget.

◆ ◆ ◆

So many things are easy to forget: the way a seed must die to grow. The way old thoughts must die for *us* to grow.

A wise person once said that when something good comes into our lives, it is either seed or bread; we either plant and cultivate it, or we enjoy and consume it.

And some magical times, we get to do both.

I have been given a writing residency here in San Francisco. Each morning, I plant myself at this desk and cultivate words. But I also enjoy the wide swaths of time to write, and I eat up the light that comes through the bay windows and the sunrises over the actual Bay. I savor the art on the walls and the books on the shelves even as I work on my own book with its own art.

What does this have to do with love?

Everything.

◆ ◆ ◆

Love is the sum of all the other eight qualities.

Love is patient, love is kind.

Love is the whole kit & caboodle.

Love is and is and is.

Love is the sum of every sacrifice made for something more than the moment in which it's made. But Love is *in* the moment, too.

And Love has fun. When she's living large on little, Love packs a picnic to bring to the park and shares it with friends.

Sure, Love could make reservations at the fancy restaurant and order the lobster—and she's done that, too, because Love can be extravagant and milestone-grand. But it seems extremely likely that Love especially loves to share herself in the little ways and the everyday days.

Joy

◆ ◆ ◆

The idea that an apple a day keeps the doctor away only works if we choose to eat the apple.

Joy is an active choice we make.

I like to distinguish happiness from joy. To me, happiness depends on a certain outcome or circumstance, but joy is independent of any externals—it's a heart-set. A choice.

This means I can still have joy in the midst of grief, but I probably can't be happy. I can be happy when I buy a new pair of boots, but not necessarily when I splatter paint all over them—and joy doesn't require any specific footwear.

But then, I sometimes forget my own theory and use happiness and joy interchangeably.

Sometimes, joy is taking a moment to laugh at ourselves and all of our theories.

[T]he mere sense of living is joy enough.
—Emily Dickinson

♦ ♦ ♦

You know those days when joy and happiness are both present? Those are the apex days, the ones that stick with you. That you can recall years and years later.

One of mine: long, long ago. State Street, Chicago. The day after Thanksgiving. The man I thought I'd marry had invited me to celebrate the holiday with his family, and we all walked downtown to see the Macy's holiday window displays. The busy sidewalks bustled with smiling, well-dressed people in their coats and scarves, and I was glad to be wearing my favorite vintage dress.[3]

The air was full of Christmas music and the scent of evergreen and the sense of hope.

That was before the circumstances arose that squelched the happiness I'd conflated with joy.

---

[3] A five-dollar, thrift-store find.

◆◆◆

I am truly grateful to that ex-boyfriend for helping me learn that joy is a choice and for inadvertently inspiring my living-large-on-little journey.[4]

It's easy to see others missing out on joy when reality falls short of their expectations; it's harder to see our own ways of pegging joy to a circumstance. I still catch myself doing it. But the examples from my ex are a bit more glamorous—he always did things with style—so just this once, I'll use someone else as an illustration....

Example 1: When I met him, he thought he'd be able to retire happy when he had 4 million in the bank. In less than a year, that desired number had increased to 20 million in a kind of happiness hedge-betting (or hedge funding).

Example 2: When we visited a Spanish olive grove, he was flipping through travel magazines and wanting to be on a tropical island. Or crossing the Strait to Morocco.

I was (and still am) a poet-painter working as a freelance editor. For much of the time we dated, I had only a few hundred dollars to my name at any one time. I quickly saw that if I waited to cultivate joy before I had even one comma in my bank account, I'd be a very unhappy person.

So thank you, dear Mr. X: I am truly grateful

---

[4] A PSA for my other ex-boyfriends who will probably never read this, but still: this will be the only time in these pages I use an ex as an illustration, so don't worry—though I have plenty of material—and I'm sure I provided plenty, too!

for that lesson. And I truly hope you've found your circumstance-free joy.

Many people lose the small joys in the hope for the big happiness.

—Pearl S. Buck

♦ ♦ ♦

Not long ago, psychologists discovered that the anticipation of an experience can increase the joy of that experience. In fact, anticipation can often be even more pleasurable than the thing being anticipated.

This helps when living large on little, because usually, planning saves money, and angst, and last-minute tromping through the rainy streets of Kuta, Bali, looking for a hotel room during winter break—but that's another story.

Planning ahead is a great way to build anticipation, and I've come to enjoy the lead-up as much as what it leads up to.

Anticipation isn't a requirement for joy, but it's a nice enhancement. It's a bit like cake: a good, dense chocolate cake is just fine all by itself. Add chocolate ganache, and it's just that much better.

To the ganache of anticipation—*bon appétit!*

◆ ◆ ◆

Gratitude and grace aren't officially fruit of the Spirit, but I like to think they are grafted into all of the fruit.

I'd love to easily afford cashmere and Champagne with a capital "C." But I can be grateful for wool and sparkling wine.

I've worn cashmere, and I've enjoyed Champagne. Beautiful things, both. They might have made me happy in the moment, but they didn't alter my joy.

What if the more we give thanks for little things in our lives, the more grace has space to bring the large?

Give thanks, take joy.

Peace

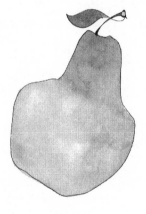

◆◆◆

During my freshman year in college, I received an invitation to attend a sales event in the conference room of a local hotel. I confess I only went for the free lunch.

I should have remembered the maxim from my high school economy class: *There's no such thing as a free lunch.*

This particular strings-attached meal was a sales pitch for some sort of lifetime discount plan, presented by a portly man in a tie more like: The Discount Plan of a LIFETIME!!!

We special students, he told us, the few who had been selected to attend,[5] had the chance to sign up then and there to become members of this miraculous Plan which would give us discounts on all of our future household items forever. For the bargain, non-refundable membership price of $2,000.

No rush, but the offer would expire as soon as the presentation was over.

The salesman was good, and I was naïve. I was also poor—putting myself through college on scholarships—and I didn't have 2K to spare. But as I sat there trying to digest the soggy hotel salad, I agonized about whether I would walk out those paneled doors regretting the lost chance to save on a future washing machine.

That Saturday afternoon was one of the first

---

[5] Translation: the few of us gullible enough to respond to the invitation.

times I made a solo financial decision as an adult—though a "seventeen-year-old adult" might be more of an oxymoron than a reality.

I couldn't explain it until many years later, but I realized that there was no peace in the decision being presented to me that day. It was a non-essential, pressure-cooker choice—the kind that makes you feel as if you'll explode if you don't make a decision *now*.

These days, if I feel pressured to buy something, I don't. I back away, right away. Especially if the thing or experience is one I hadn't even thought of before the sales pitch.

And I have never yet had to buy a brand-new washing machine.

◆ ◆ ◆

Marketers, bless their talented hearts, know how to be elegant and subtle, too. They know how to spin a gentle story about that organic, fair-trade, shade-grown product that will smooth its way into our dreams and melt all our fears of aging.

I have nothing against marketing in general, but I don't like fear-based marketing. Generally, I just want to be fully aware of why I'm being sold something and how I'm reacting to the sales pitch.

But many marketers consciously work the *slow* cooker of pressure: the social media ads that recur, the newsletter that offers continual sales on the item we eventually can't imagine our lives without.

Therein the rub: our beautiful-but-oft-coopted imagination.

An idea: you know the practice of blessing meals before eating them?[6] What if we blessed our imagination? How would that impact our spirit's ability to process the stimuli the world hurls at us?

It might go something like this: we'd see a glossy ad for the latest beauty product, but

---

[6] I hope there is a scientific study somewhere to support the idea that blessing our food is good for us, but if not, here's a poet's science: Dr. Masuro Emoto's famous study of water showed, at the microscopic level, what happens to water molecules when exposed to various labels. Look up his work, and you can see the difference between water labeled "love" vs. "hate." Most interesting when we remember that our bodies are mostly water.

instead of feeling lack for not having it, we might remember that book of beauty secrets we once read and how an oat-honey mask does wonders for the skin—much the same wonders that the Very Expensive Skin Crème promises. And what do you know? We happen to have oatmeal and honey in our cupboards right now.

Of course, many times, a company has great intentions, a wonderful product, and is doing some beautiful civic or environmental work, like helping people with mental illness find jobs or funding reforestation. Bravo.

But living large on little means mostly cutting out the middle man, so for now, I'll stick with oats and honey, and I'll send a check to Living Opportunities.[7]

Who knows, you might find the fancy jar of wonder crème in my medicine cabinet someday. But probably not while I'm living large on little.

[7] Living Opportunities is a big-hearted, many-faceted local organization that helps people with developmental disabilities find jobs and also offers access to The Studio where they can create art.

Being requires limitation.

—Jordan Peterson

◆ ◆ ◆

On this journey, it helps to differentiate between needs and wants. Food is the best example I've found—and the reason you'll find so many references to it in this book.

I need to eat. I don't need to eat at a restaurant, though I might want to. I don't need to buy imported pears wrapped individually in tissue at the equivalent of Dean & DeLuca, though I might want to. [8] I can choose to plant a patio garden and shop at the farmers' market or the locally owned discount grocer's.

And I find that when I make peace with the need-want distinction, I can deviate from it consciously instead of unconsciously.

Now and then I do splurge on the imported mascarpone and Belgian chocolate. But as I've been practicing living large on little over the years, I've found a new kind of want: I *want* to find creative ways to spend less so that I can save for things that matter more.

---

[8] Interesting: as I was double-checking the spelling of this store, I discovered that they are closing this year due to excessive debt. Hmmm....

◆ ◆ ◆

These days, I am more interested in contributing to my retirement account and donating to charities than I am in going out for several nights on the town each week. If I made more money, I might do all of the above. Then again….

For a very brief period in my younger life, I used to go out. A lot. And I did *not* make a lot of money. Which meant I saved pretty much nothing for anything longer term than the next trip I wanted to take.

Truthfully? It felt more like living little on little—I had no wide-scope lens for my future. Plus, a party lifestyle starts to feel less glamorous once wrinkles begin to appear and you realize your liver isn't going to be twenty three forever.

In my defense, the frontal lobe of the human brain—the "control panel"—doesn't fully develop until about age 25, so we can blame many faulty, first-quarter-of-life decisions on physiology.[9]

But then again, I made a stupid decision just the other day, so what can I say, other than that the number and density of dumb decisions thankfully diminishes as we embrace grace with gratitude.

My needs-wants relationship has, like my brain, grown up. For the most part, I choose to do things that bring me peace—because plenty of

---

[9] Rental car agencies have figured out frontal-lobe development; there's a reason they charge people under age 25 a "young renter" fee. And yet we can drive cars, drink in bars, and fight in wars well before that. I digress.

things I *don't* choose fling themselves at me with built-in chaos.

Will taking that trip take away from the savings contribution I committed to?

Yes.

Will that bring me peace?

No.

Then I won't go.

What if we consistently asked ourselves: will the fruit of this decision bring peace? If it won't, there is likely another decision that will, and we can invite our imagination to help find it.

And hey, one less round of jetlag and jet fuel is probably a good thing.[10]

---

[10] I say this having helped lead travel writing workshops for over five years. I still love travel: I'm just extra aware of why I'm going and whether I'm confusing activity with identity.

Patience

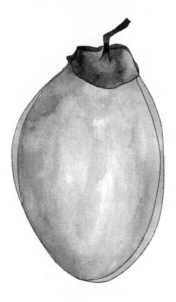

◆ ◆ ◆

When I taught high school on a tiny, Micronesian island, far, far away, I learned to make weekends sacred. I tried to get out and enjoy the ocean, which was my favorite thing to do there.

One Saturday morning, I stopped at the local outdoor market and bought a coconut to take to Wings Beach. With any luck, I'd have that northern nook of the island to myself. It was an unprotected beach, as in: no coral reef to create a lagoon and keep the sharks out. I was always a bit afraid of swimming in those waters, and I would force myself to do it.[11]

My car lurched down the pocked, coral road, and I arrived to—delight!—a deserted beach.

I laid out my sarong on the sand and sipped the coconut juice through the straw sticking from the hole that the man at the market had machete'd open for me. When I finished the juice, I thought: *I want to eat the coconut meat inside.* But this was the entire coconut—thick, green outer casing and all.

Limitation: I had no machete.

Invitation: How else can I open it?

I will not admit how long it took me to break

---

[11] In my early thirties, I made it a goal to consciously conquer my fears. Here are the top three at that time: 1) public speaking. Solution: teach high school. 2) Going to China alone. Solution: go to China alone. 3) SCUBA diving. Solution: get PADI certified—even if I hope to never again use that certification!

that thing open. It involved much hefting and not a few rounds of bashing against rocks. I'm glad there were no witnesses but the coconut crabs, scuttling for cover.

When I finally heard that shell crack in half, I felt an ancient thrill that no modern equipment of convenience can give.

I sat on my sarong and scooped out the coconut meat. I ate it with revelry, facing the sea and sky in their many hues of blue.

When I had scraped out the last of the sweet fruit, I stacked the two shells and ran my hands through the sand—sand that had once been stone or coral and was now soft enough to comfortably sit on.

So much is worth waiting for.

Sometimes, that waiting is passive, but many times, it's a muscle'd waiting, filled with sweat and repetition like the tides. Or the sound of continuous thudding of coconut on stone.

Patience is also a form of action.
                                    —Auguste Rodin

◆ ◆ ◆

Though I spent most of my childhood in Montana, our family moved away when I was ten, and we lived several other places before I returned to the State to attend university.

To fund my education, I spent hours in a dark room, deep beneath the admissions office, on a pre-Google database of scholarships, grants, and internships. I applied for anything and everything, and I'm so grateful that I was able to make it through all of my education without debt.[12]

It was on one of those financial aid searches that I discovered the world of paid internships. Which is how I came to apply to intern at The Cloisters—the medieval branch of The Metropolitan Museum of Art in New York.

This was back when rejections and acceptances arrived via snail mail—sometimes a

---

[12] A bit of a sidebar here....The brief era of "party Anna" I mentioned earlier did not begin until graduate school. Up through my undergraduate years, I was Little Miss Studious. I filled my life with school and work, and the rare parties I went to were events like Thanksgiving dinners at the Hutterite colony and art receptions at the Yellowstone Art Museum where I volunteered as a docent. That conscientious me knew that to graduate with debt and a double degree in English and Art would lay a heavy burden on her art. She was right—but I wish she'd made a bit more time to have fun. Now, when I think about my future self, I try to do the things that will serve her best—but I also try to enjoy the moment with my present self. And I leave some room for grace to do its work, too.

phone call for the latter.

For most of my undergraduate years, I rented a tiny basement apartment off campus for less than the cost of the dorms. If I wasn't in class or at work, I was at home studying. In the afternoons, I would often see the mailman's legs as he passed the external stairwell and deposited my letters in the vintage metal mail box mounted to the wall of the main house. I'd hear the clink of the little lid, see the legs disappear, and then bolt out my door and up the stairs to see what news might have arrived.

One day, there came a letter from New York. It was an invitation to interview for The Cloisters internship. In person.

Herein the condensed version of what took months: I asked a trusted professor for guidance, and he helped me find university funding to fly from Montana to New York. I got on a plane—my first time traveling long distance completely alone—landed at JFK, taxied to my hotel in Manhattan, and cried myself to sleep to the foreign soundtrack of five-part car alarms. The next morning, I gave myself an extra hour to get to my interview, which was good, because I took the wrong bus and arrived to the museum in Fort Tryon Park with one minute to spare. I interviewed, petrified. But I did it. I came back to my hotel and this time did *not* cry. The next day, I flew home to Montana. Eventually, I received a call; I had been accepted to the internship, along with seven other students from around the country. I was elated. I finished the semester, got on another plane, and flew back to New York where I would spend the summer learning about medieval history, giving tours to day campers, and preparing a gallery talk to deliver to a public audience—the culmination of the internship.

That overlong paragraph does not convey the wait between mailing off my application and receiving the phone call of acceptance—let alone arriving to New York to begin the internship.

I like instant gratification as much as the next person, but I have to say, there is something about building a history with patience. If I were a financial advisor, I'd talk about its usefulness when it comes to compound interest.

But my poet's note on patience here is one of compound gratitude: I am grateful for those years of applying for things and waiting to hear the results—most of which were rejections— because I quickly learned not to attach all my hopes to any one, single outcome.

And I am grateful I was able to spend a summer working amid buildings made of ancient stones brought over land and sea and reassembled on a bluff at the northern end of Manhattan.

That setting taught me how fleeting my idea of "a long time" really is. It also taught me that the things we build might end up looking different than we intended—or provide us with a different vantage point from when we first began.

Lessons I am still learning.

To fly, we have to have resistance.

—Maya Lin

◆◆◆

When I lived in Germany, a friend asked if I wanted to travel to India with her to help work in an orphanage.

After a year of writing poetry on a fellowship at an art center in Karlsruhe, I had stayed on as an intern. I received a small, monthly stipend; it was just enough to pay my sublet rent and attend a few too many *Biergarten* gatherings. But once I had the goal of going to India, I nixed the gatherings and slashed my grocery bill.

Fun fact: the German equivalent of the English phrase "starving artist" is *brotlos*, or breadless. Yet bread just happens to be the most affordable and plentiful grocery item in Germany. I ended up eating a lot of it to save money.

The art center where I worked had a massive communal kitchen available to all employees, and after receptions, leftover food would be set out on the counter for anyone to take. I kept track of all the events and was the first one to scavenge.

In less than six months, I'd saved enough for my airline ticket and incidentals for forty days in a small, Indian town between Bangalore and Chennai—on an intern's stipend.

I don't recommend a diet of bread and remnants, but hey, I was young. And I learned the power of patience paired with rethinking my existing circumstances.

◆◆◆

I won't write about India here because it's part of such an oft-told travel tale: journey to a developing country, help out in an orphanage, and learn just how privileged you really are— even if you live below your own country's poverty line. Like most clichés, it's true.

But harder for me has been living in my own country in poverty.

When I returned to the US from teaching in Micronesia, I did so right smack in the middle of The Great Recession. I left a secure job to study at a school of ministry in Redding, California (like many of my asides, that's another story).

I had saved just enough to attend one year of the school, but I ended up staying for all three.

The second year was hard. By that time, the only place I could afford to rent was an unplumbed cabin in a run-down neighborhood on an unmaintained "street" that was more of an extended dirt rut with deep potholes.

I had a key to the main house, which let me access the bathroom and kitchen.

If I came home on a rainy night and forgot my headlamp, I would practice my night vision as I descended the cement walk into the large, forested yard to reach my little cabin, which had no central heat or air conditioning. A wall unit purportedly provided both, but I was asked to not leave it on when I was away from the property, which meant I usually arrived to a stifling hot room or a freezing cold one.

I could find no part-time work while attending the school that year, even near the holidays. So, just before Christmas, I decided I'd give up searching for paid work and start on my own work in addition to my required studies.

And so it began that I started writing poetry again—something I hadn't made much time for in years.

I wrote, and I wrote. I spent my dawns with coffee and God, watching light break through the forest. I began sending poetry out to journals and getting it published. It was a season of active waiting.

By late winter, I had an idea: if I couldn't find part-time work while in school, I'd make my own. So I started to create a six-week poetry workshop. Then I contacted the Shasta County Arts Council and asked if I could use one of their classrooms. I plastered the town with flyers and told everyone I knew in the area about the poetry course.

I ended up with three whole students. Though it was a teensy class, it was fun, and I made enough money to keep the tank of my car filled with gas that semester.

That was the first poetry workshop I created outside of academia. It was the workshop that set in motion all the others I've taught since.

Just this summer, I was invited to teach poetry in Switzerland—all expenses covered. That might never have happened had I not chosen to find the invitation in my limitation a decade ago.

By the time I started my third year at that school of ministry, I had a job as an adjunct professor of English at the local university. And by that final spring, I began to receive jobs for content editing—freelance work which I've been doing ever since.

I once read a bit of advice that I have searched high and low to find and credit. Failing that, I'll paraphrase it here: every writer should spend a year working in a poor room. That's not sexy advice. But it might just be *good* advice.

Cheers to patience. And to being retro-grateful for that time working in a dingy little one-room cabin—if only so that I never again have to work in a dingy little one-room cabin.

Kindness

♦♦♦

Be kind

Before I started my brief high-school teaching career, I had to take a batch of subject-matter competency tests. They were administered by our local university on a Saturday morning, and I felt like *I* was in high school again as I waited in line with the young students there to take their college placement exams.

After hours of penciling in answers on Scantron sheets, I rewarded myself with brunch at a nearby café.

The dining room was completely full. When a server showed me to the last free seat at the bar, I exhaled with relief. Then I inhaled the scent of bacon, maple, and butter. I drooled over the menu, noticing that the woman to my right was also solo and also drooling over her menu. We traded sighs of delight, "O, the peach pancakes!" And "O, the rock shrimp omelets!"

We ended up eating alone together, having a wonderful conversation. She discovered that I was going to begin teaching, and I discovered that she had just finished a career in teaching.

As I reveled in the pat of butter sliding down my pancake in a run of peach sauce, I asked her, "What is the one thing you hoped all of your students learned?

Without missing a beat, she said, "Be nice. I wanted them to learn to be nice."

I've never forgotten that. It was a holy

moment there in the crowded restaurant—two strangers connecting over the ultimate lesson plan.

I long ago altered the phrase "be nice" to "be kind," if only because "nice" tends to get a bad rap. Kindness seems sturdier to me.

And kindness plays several roles in living large on little....

Be kind to yourself

Several years ago, I decided to give up financial insecurity for Lent.[13]

Every day, for forty days, I committed to actively studying personal finance for a minimum of an hour—two hours if I could swing it. This was in addition to working on a massive content editing project, prepping for my twenty-year painting retrospective, and launching a little "children's book for grownups."[14] I definitely took on a bit too much at once, but it reminded me that there's always time to learn.

I checked out financial books from my local library, listened to podcasts, and played with online calculators. By Easter, I had opened a Roth IRA. I had an idea of my "number," the amount I needed to have saved by the time I retire to maintain my current lifestyle—not as much as I'd dreaded. But the most meaningful outcome of that Lenten adventure was the new confidence that I could continue to make a life as an artist, even if I never made a big "living."

I felt like I had become my own ally. Taking that time to study something that had slightly scared me—or at the very least made me feel completely inadequate—was an act of financial

---

[13] I don't practice Catholicism, but I love many of its traditions.

[14] *And: The Story of More*

kindness to myself.

Now, I try to do at least one new, comfort-zone-stretching thing each year with my finances. Two years ago, I finally got a fiduciary advisor. Just this year, I finally automated my savings— something I told myself I could skip because of erratic income. But being kind to ourselves can look like being firm. Like saying to our scared, four-year-old selves on the way to kindergarten: *Yes, you have to go to school. But guess what? You'll make new friends. You'll learn new things. And you'll be glad you went.*

And, if you're a freelancing poet-painter, you might even end up with enough to retire.

◆ ◆ ◆

Be kind to others

We all know the adage: love your neighbor as yourself. What if not loving our neighbors well— whether they're next door or across the border— actually stems from not loving ourselves well? If we love others badly, it's very likely we're loving ourselves badly—which, among other things, will probably also result in bad financial decisions.

Nothing can make our life, or the lives of other people, more beautiful than perpetual kindness.

—Leo Tolstoy

◆ ◆ ◆

Be kind to the planet

We vote with our dollars; what we buy determines what is made, and how. Voting with our dollars can be good—but it can also be hard if we're living large on little.

Often, the least expensive option isn't the best for the environment. This can appear to be a limitation, but like all limitations, it can also be an invitation.

I start where I can, and since I love creative recycling, that's my main expression of environmentalism at the moment.

The wood flooring in my little loft was once old barn siding from the nearby Applegate Valley. My standing desk and book case is repurposed oak shelving from our historic Carnegie libraries—bought for a song when Jackson County sold off the old shelves and built new, larger libraries.[15]

Most of my clothing is second hand and/or free—either from clothing swaps, friends who have practiced the "magic of tidying up" their closets,[16] or resale shops where I maintain continual store credit by recycling my wardrobe.

And then there's the trade system. I'm not sure if this counts as being kind to the

---

[15] With enormous gratitude to my family who transformed and installed those repurposed things for me!

[16] With enormous gratitude to those friends…and to Marie Kondo!

environment, but I have traded many paintings for goods and services over the years. I keep a list, and I include some of it here for fun:

- Sheetrock installation for my loft
- A series of 10 massages
- A flight to Kalispell, Montana, on a private plane
- A session of laser hair removal
- A new, 8' x 10' wool rug from India
- Computer hard disk recovery
- Nine days of camping on private land near a tributary of the Wallowa River in Joseph, Oregon
- Poetry editing
- A week-long stay in a *riad* in Marrakech, Morocco
- Two professional photo shoots
- Website building & development
- Catering for my parents' 45th anniversary party (including enough lamb meatballs and individual panna cottas for 70+)

Whenever I add to this list, I glance back at previous trades and smile. It reminds me to think outside the box—which may well be kindness toward the environment after all.

Any time we expand our imagination, we get better at coming up with new solutions for old problems—whether relatively little ones like a crashed laptop or larger ones like making those laptops out of materials that won't damage our planet.

What if renewed imagination leads to renewable energy? If so, cultivating the imagination just might be an act of environmentalism.

Consuming less certainly is.

Goodness

◆◆◆

What fun to discover this definition of goodness: "The nutritious, flavorful, or beneficial part of something."[17]

One hindrance to that goodness is our negativity bias. Our dear brains are programmed to look for the bad. Many eons ago, this was so that we could scan an environment for threats and be able to run from lions and tigers and bears. To survive, we had to be able to process danger, and fast.

These days, few of us are running from carnivorous fauna on a regular basis—but we're on the constant lookout for its equivalent. We're wired to notice the bad more than the good.

Add to that a certain bit of long-misunderstood widsom: that all things work for good. This line has often been mis-taught from the angle that all things—bad things included—are good. They are not. From the failed exam to the death of a loved one and anywhere in between, those events in themselves are *not* good. But the key is finding how they can work *toward* good. When the bad happens, how can we interpret it? How can we transform it?

You might say that some parts of life—call them bad if you wish—are in their bitter, pre-ripe stage. We can either stay in that bitter stage, or we can invite the lessons to continue to mature in

---

[17] *Merriam-Webster,* s.v. "Goodness," www.merriamwebster.com/dictionary/goodness.

us. If we do, we might someday taste the nutritious, flavorful, beneficial part of them.

♦♦♦

It can take a bit of imagination to see goodness in an empty pantry—or one mostly filled with stale cereal.

When I arrived to this residency here in San Francisco, I brought some basic groceries with me. I'd been traveling for a week already, so I didn't have anything fresh.

The closest grocery store in this Noe Valley neighborhood is a high-end chain nicknamed Whole Paycheck.

Before walking down the five blocks to buy some produce,[18] I set out the food I'd brought and surveyed the contents of the cupboards. The latter were bulging with random dry goods left by previous residents, from peanut butter to take-out chili flakes, expired boxes of Honey Nut Cheerios to a bag of hand-made granola from a local bakery, unopened.

Two of the three bottles of olive oil smelled iffy, but one still had the fragrance of the grove.

Here was a fun challenge, especially since food is my kind of limitation-as-invitation.

---

[18] I had decided to only walk everywhere while in the city— no driving, no public transport even. I'm still a country girl at heart, and cities can overwhelm me. But the way I've found to love them is to walk and walk and walk. And when I give myself the challenge (limitation) of only walking, I reset my levels of convenience, inviting myself to appreciate the errands I run back home—which can otherwise become all too familiar and drudgy (and though that isn't a word, I think it should be!).

After making a mental note of everything usable, I walked to the grocery store. Checking the sales and specials and store-brand items, I resisted the alluring-but-expensive baskets of cherries and came home with kale, grapes, a lime, two bags of frozen broccoli florets, a block of cheddar, eggs, and half-and-half for the coffee I rarely travel without.

Back at the studio, I made a salad dressing with the good olive oil and chili flakes from the cupboard, the lime I'd bought, and the garlic I'd brought with me. I chopped the kale into ribbons and massaged it with the dressing. I let the greens sit while I toasted the walnuts, which I'd also brought from home. I halved the grapes, sprinkled on some parmesan I'd found hidden behind another box of cereal, and then tossed everything together. I ended up with a salad large enough for two, so I put away half of it and then sat on the little balcony to eat the other half.

Sure, I could have bought pine nuts or some fancy goat cheese to sprinkle on top of the salad. But I actually love the creative challenge of what a friend calls "cream of third shelf." It's the ability to see a random assortment of pantry items and find some new way to use them.

I imagine that many great culinary dishes grew out of some level of limitation. Like *cioppino*—the tomato-based seafood stew that originated here in San Francisco. Some savvy fisherfolk once tossed surplus fish parts into a tomato sauce and concocted what has now become an iconic North Beach specialty—one my grandfather learned to make when he worked on Treasure Island in the 1930s.

But back to choosing joy: I could lament stale Cheerios or find the goodness in chili flakes.

I enjoyed the leftover salad with eggs the next day and the broccoli with cheddar the day after that. In fact, with some resourceful combinations, I didn't have to buy any more groceries the rest of that week.

Sometimes, I do splurge on spendy cherries and similar treats. But for now, the cherry I most want to enjoy is the cherry-on-top experience of being able to work in the Bay Area for two weeks, hold a literary salon and art exhibit, and return home with money in my pocket.[19]

A challenge, yes. But such challenges are delightful when they work. To my own astonishment, for every trip I've taken this year, I've returned home with more money than when I left. That includes helping lead workshops in Mexico, Spain, Morocco, and Napa; teaching poetry in Switzerland (with a dip into Germany); a week on the Oregon Coast (housesitting), a road trip to Montana (helping at a friend's catering company and selling books at a poetry reading), and finally, this time in the Bay Area.

I am still marveling about this. It seems crazy—but then grace often does.

---

[19] Happy news: I did! During the salon and exhibit at the end of my residency, I sold my entire collection of word-paintings along with prints and a few books. In the end, I more than covered all of my expenses and even made a bit of profit.

I continually remind myself that most anything is doable with a mix of planning, spontaneity, and imagination.

✦✦✦

When I lived in Germany, I applied for a big grant from the art center where I worked. This grant would have provided me with enough money to live and work another year in the country.

I stressed about the presentation for days. I thought the source of my anxiety was the expectation that I would give my presentation in German. I had been in the country for almost two years, and I spoke the language proficiently but only conversationally. Larger, abstract ideas were still hard for me to convey.

I didn't realize I was actually suffering from an extended case of imposter syndrome—the symptoms of which had been obvious from the minute I'd been give my own corner office. I had sat in front of my issued computer and worried that the art center would figure out I wasn't as cool as the electroacoustic composers or New Media artists who dressed in hipster, GDR-era jackets and traveled to neighboring countries to set up interactive digital installations or to DJ and VJ private parties.[20]

The day of the proposals arrived. The grant committee convened the three of us applicants in a large conference room on the top floor of the massive arts complex. The other two applicants were my friends.

I ended up presenting in English out of

---

[20] I didn't even know that a VJ was a video-jockey.

64

panic, but I did as badly as if I had tried to present in German. I didn't believe in myself. I didn't believe I was good enough.

And I didn't receive the grant.

It was split between my two friends, as if to confirm that I was, indeed, *not* good enough.

Odd thing: that external rejection triggered something in me. It took me a few years to put words to it, but I finally began to see that what people thought of me—good or bad—had nothing to do with my value.

Goodness is an inside job. Such knowledge was worth more than that lost grant.

◆ ◆ ◆

Last July, I took a sabbatical. I had never taken an entire month off as a grown-up, and it was weird and wonderful.[21] I technically *was* working on a poetry manuscript, but poetry is my delight, so it didn't feel like work.

In the afternoons, when I would have normally been catching up on my interminable to-do list, I started reading books from my childhood. Stacks of Little Golden Books and fairy tales by the Brothers Grimm piled up by my hammock.

Toward the end of my sabbatical, I read *Cinderella*. As a forty-something now, I saw the story from an entirely new light—a kind of re-vision; I identified with the fairy godmother, not the princess-to-be.

I began to dream about how much more marvelous it would be to wield the wand and grant goodness than just wait to receive it.

The morning after my sabbatical ended, I received news that I had been accepted for a writing residency in Vermont. Elation!

Allow me to pause here.

I have an unofficial rule about travel for professional development, lest I justify myself into expenses—even if they are tax write-offs. (And I never, ever put anything on a credit card that I can't pay off at the end of each month.) At

---

[21] I'm always surprised at how much work it can be to *not* work!

66

least two of these three categories need to be covered for me to go:

1. Transportation
2. Fees/tuition
3. Accommodation

I knew I had enough frequent flyer miles saved up for just such an opportunity,[22] so that left the other two categories.

The residency awarded me a partial artist grant, which was wonderful, but this bill was a bit bigger than that of the usual week-long workshops I attend.

So I sent out a newsletter, announcing the residency and inviting people to purchase my books, art, cards, etc. The response was over-whelming—and included generous donations. Within days, the rest of the residency bill was entirely covered.

One of the hardest parts of living large on little has been balancing effort with grace. I am continually reminded that our personal limitations can be invitations for grace, if we let them.

Sometimes we get to be the fairy godmother, and sometimes we get to be on the receiving end of her Bibbedi-Bobbedi-Boo. Goodness works from every direction.

---

[22] My round-trip flight from Oregon to Vermont on frequent-flier miles cost me $11.20 in taxes and surcharges. I call that free!

Here's to blessing and being blessed by the sparkling wand of the possible.

Where there is kindness, there is goodness. And where there is goodness, there is magic.

—Cinderella

Faithfulness

Being faithful in the smallest things is the way to gain, maintain, and demonstrate the strength needed to accomplish something great.

—Alex Harris

◆◆◆

I've read a lot of books and listened to a lot of teachings on finance. So much information. So many particulars. It all boggles.

Some of the best macro advice about money I ever heard came from a wise CPA. He suggested that we think of our money in three categories: Living, Giving, and Saving.

Simple. I like that.

Even more, I like that his goal was to shift his percentages from the living category toward the other two.

Say you start with a ratio of 80-10-10; that's 80% for living, 10% for giving, 10% for saving. The aim is to move more into the giving and saving categories. He and his wife had moved near 50-25-25. Their target ratio? To live off only 10% of their income and then save and give away the rest. How beautiful. And how different from most investment advice.

That goal takes a lot of faithfulness. It also takes a lot of imaginative thinking—like asking ourselves what we can do for the world if we're giving more than we're taking.

We make a living by what we get, but we make a life by what we give.

—Winston Churchill

◆◆◆

As a natural saver, you'd think I'd love budgets. Problem is: I've been freelancing for many, many years, and my income is erratic. I can technically create a baseline budget based on averages, and I do, but…life happens. And so do out-of-pocket periodontic surgeries (may you never need a gum graft!).

I do set a grocery budget, since eating is one of the few, true needs in this life. Some years, like this one, I lump all food into this budget—dining out included.

This can pose a problem when I'm invited to eat out at restaurants. I often decline. Mostly for financial reasons. But also, the average restaurant isn't using organic food, mineral-rich sea salt, cold-pressed olive oil, etc.[23] I can buy these things inexpensively when I'm home, because I know where to shop for them. When I travel…well, that's another section.

Back to declining the dinner invitation. Another alternative is to accept—but to only order a beverage. This idea grew out of practicing a kind of intermittent fasting most days of the week.[24] Since I usually don't eat after 5 PM, the dinner invitation was a bit of a lose-lose: I'd walk

---

[23] I know there are splendid restaurants out there that do. Every few blue moons, I do dine somewhere fine, and it's all the more marvelous for the rarity.

[24] Which I started doing over a decade ago, long before I knew it had a name. I just thought of it as the "I sleep soooo much better when I'm not full" strategy.

away feeling bloated *and* broke. I'd rather keep my waistline thin and my wallet fat.

Now and then, I do enjoy dinner—even dinner at a restaurant. It can be delightful to meet up with friends at a local eatery and savor blueberry sauce over tenderloin. But if I want 80-year old me to be able to afford groceries—let alone dining out—then I choose those times deliberately.

It helps when I think of it less like I'm losing out on an experience now and more like I'm saving for an experience later. Admittedly, there is a balance between enjoying the moment and planning for future moments, but faithfulness to a long-term vision helps me build a history of trust with myself—a win-win when living large on little.[25]

---

[25] And for the times that aren't a win-win, there's thankfully grace!

◆ ◆ ◆

I started to write this section about sticking to a budget while traveling, but while mulling over the forty countries I've visited, I couldn't agree with myself.

Twenty-four hours in Iceland cost me more than two weeks in Nepal, and travel for work is different from personal travel.

I decided I liked my list of subtitle ideas better than what I started to write for each of them. So here's what this section could have been about:

- Creating a travel budget
- The illusion of the travel budget
- How to stick to your budget when traveling
- What to do when you break your travel budget
- Happy hour in Italy!
- Happy hour anywhere!
- Free museums in Paris
- Art receptions & charcuterie boards
- Markets: street markets, farmers markets, & flea markets
- Luxury housesitting
- Any housesitting!
- How I flew to Japan (and New Zealand, and Germany, and, and, and...) for free

But what this section would really be about is using our imaginations to find ways to travel for cheap or for free—both of which are possible.

Entire blogospheres career with particulars on how to do this. I like to read those blogs. But I also like to think beyond the concrete and the calculated. To pay attention to existing opportunities in my life. To listen. To ask questions. One conversation around a dinner table and another while volunteering turned into mostly free trips to Chile and Ireland, respectively.[26]

And if none of this seems relevant to faithfulness, the connection is this: when we are faithful to continually push into and past our limitations, to turn our little into large, opportunities are more likely to find us.

---

[26] I realize that if I didn't travel, I'd save a lot more money—even on inexpensive or mostly free trips. But I'm not trying to live *little* on little. Travel has long been one of my great loves, and living large on little is about finding ways to do the big things we love, even with limited resources—which usually requires letting go of other things.

♦ ♦ ♦

As I mentioned in my opening gratitude, I am working on this book while staying in San Francisco—a city that often claims the dubious honor of being the most expensive city in the United States.

Yesterday, I walked a couple of miles to the Tartine Bakery in the Mission, passing pastel Victorian houses and young trees in their sidewalk planters—part of the city's Urban Forest Plan. It was a beautiful way to build up an appetite.

I'd heard about Tartine for years, and I was happy to see that there was still a line out the door. Always a good sign.

While I waited, I scanned the menu, deciding on something small and savory. The *gougère*, which I'm sure I mispronounced when I ordered it, sounded like a delicious marriage of *gruyère* and pepper.

I've mentioned that I rarely eat out. Bakeries are a great compromise: I get a little something special without all the extra expenses. Still, with tip, the price of that fancy pastry cost the equivalent of my normal daily grocery budget.

I took my "meal" to go, since the bakery was packed and loud, and I walked to Mission Dolores Park.

I found a bench in the shade looking down across the city. Below me on the playground, well-dressed children romped within a few feet of their hovering parents. Where the park lined

Dolores Street, tent encampments of the homeless dotted the grass.

I opened my little brown bakery bag and took a bite. The pastry was beautiful. Worth it, even.

Then a cluster of thoughts flitted across me like the leafy shade:

1. Am I a terrible person for sitting here eating an expensive pastry while the homeless are clustered down the hill? Should I go back and buy another *gougère* to give away? If so, to whom? There are so many....

2. I have no idea whether that well-coiffed woman with the tow-headed toddler on the swing set is any happier than the swarthy man in a sleeping bag near his shopping cart packed full of garbage bags, smiling up at the sky.

3. If I had agreed to marry that wealthy beau once upon a time, would I be having this thought? Or would I be the well-coiffed woman on the playground contemplating divorce?

4. I am responsible for my own joy, which is not continent upon budgets (existing, kept, or broken). Or baked goods.

5. Can I just enjoy my pastry already?

Welcome to the embarrassment of an imagination fail. I'm getting better at avoiding it, but it's an old thought spiral I'm still working to revise. Thankfully, this instance only lasted from numbers 1 through 3, at which point I realized I was wasting a wonderful moment by living in the past and the future.

I snapped out of it. I said "Thank you," aloud to the sky. I took another bite of my *gougère*, concentrating on its texture and flavor—the soft center, crusty exterior, surprise of pepper flakes. I let myself feel the pleasure of finally making it to a place I'd long wanted to visit.

It's taken me a while to be present in the moment. It helps when I express gratitude and consciously note what I am experiencing with my five senses. Because what's the point of saving for special moments if I don't enjoy them? That's a danger of living *for* a goal instead of *from* it.

After the last greasy flakes of pastry had fallen into my lap, I stood, dusted myself off, and started back to this desk, to these words.

Hopefully, the next time I treat myself to a little splurge, I'll be better able to straight up enjoy it.

Sometimes, the trajectory of faithfulness looks like getting a little bit better at each failure.

Gentleness

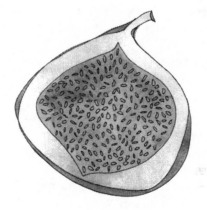

◆ ◆ ◆

And now for gentleness. This one is vital for living large on little because failure, like death and taxes, is an inevitable part of life. I try to embrace failure as part of the learning curve—though sometimes I fail to do so!

Here's an example. When I told a couple of friends about this book idea, they suggested I buy the domain name for a future website.

I did some online coupon hunting and found a good deal via a web hosting site. I had to create an account and sign in to complete the purchase, and when I did, the coupon disappeared. Zero discount.

Sigh.

Part of living large is knowing when to let the littles go. Where I once would have spent half an hour with customer service trying to get the coupon post-purchase, I decided to call "taco."

I can thank an old acquaintance for this concept. Back around the millennium, I was in Baja with a brilliant batch of alumni from a Very Illustrious Technical School. We were all staying in a massive yurt. Long story.

One afternoon, we all went out for tacos. I was debating whether or not to buy a little silver ring I'd seen in the *mercado*. Lauren asked how much it was. When I told her, she said, "Oh honey, that's just a few fish tacos."

Back to The Case of the Disappearing Coupon….

I let it go.

More tacos: a few days after purchasing the domain, I realized that, in fact, I did not want to build and maintain yet another website, so I cancelled it—not realizing that the window for reimbursement had closed.

I lost maybe the equivalent of a dozen tacos, so this was no tragedy. Still. I would rather have donated that money to one of my favorite local charities than have thrown it at a giant domain company.

But gentleness.

When I start to lament or bemoan lost littles, I often hear Lauren's voice on a balmy day on the Sea of Cortez: "Oh, honey. That's just a few fish tacos."

Mistakes are the portals of discovery.
                                    —James Joyce

◆◆◆

It has been grand to be in San Francisco in August. Back home in Southern Oregon, the temperatures hover near 100°. Here, even with a few toasty days, I've been surprised; what starts out as a warm, almost-hot morning cools in the afternoon as the coastal breezes roll over Twin Peaks and on toward the East Bay.[27]

One limitation I struggle with each year: the heat of August. Heat is inescapable to me. Cold I can layer against.

I also struggle in the heat of summer because I love to write in the mornings and walk in the afternoons. If it's already 80 degrees by 8 am, I end up breaking the writing flow to go for my vital, daily walk. (I know—If that's my major problem this month, then life is pretty good!)

But this weather by the Bay has been a gift: hot, still mornings when I'm happy to stay in and write. Then a midday breeze that gathers speed until it's a full, cooling wind, and I can walk for miles without breaking a sweat.

After writing this morning, I made a simple lunch of steamed broccoli with cheddar and took it to the little metal table and chair on the balcony. Theoretically, there would be a sweeping view of downtown and the East Bay, but a massive tree I couldn't find in the *Northern California Nature Guide* has grown to obscure

---

[27] Though I might have the wind direction backward...you don't want me captaining a sail boat!

most of the horizon. My main view is of the hill between Diamond and Castro, and I find it oddly mesmerizing to watch the city busses brake down the steepness of Castro Street and disappear around 24th.

In the garden below the balcony grows a fig tree. Right about noon, the branches of both trees begin to quiver. An hour later, they'll begin to sway, and for the rest of the afternoon, they'll dance in the brisk wind.

As I ate my broccoli, watching the breeze begin, I remembered learning the difference between windfall and drop; fallen apples are called windfall on the West Coast and drops in the East.

I spent last October in the little town of Johnson, Vermont, on a writing residency. October in Vermont is all about apples and cider. While there, another resident invited me to join her in Burlington for a proper apple pressing. I declined—not because I didn't want to go, but because I only had a month to work on my poetry manuscript, and I was right in the middle of a thematic breakthrough.

I had this odd feeling that if I let myself sit and watch the Gihon River run past my studio window, the solution would come without my forcing it.

And it did.

We can work so hard to make things happen—and often we *do* need to work hard. We can also play hard. Other times, maybe we need to sit and watch the afternoon wind begin to shimmy a fig tree. To imagine when the now-green fruit will be so ripe the wind will shake it loose.

Sometimes life is struggle, and sometimes it is windfall.

Self-Control

◆◆◆

I have a hunch that hedonic adaptation is the archenemy of self-control. Hedonic adaptation (also known as hedonic creep or the hedonic treadmill) is the idea that we have a baseline of happiness, and after we consume a new thing or experience, we get used to it and return to our baseline of happiness.

We discover Meyer lemons, which elevate our ordinary lemon bar recipe into heavenly delight...until the third time we make a batch, and we don't even notice. Or we are given a designer jacket that, when we first don it, makes us feel ready for our close up, but by next season feels as hum-drum as the old jacket we had before it.

Each new thing or experience becomes our new normal. So we crave something newer, and *that* thing becomes normal, and...the beat goes on.

What if consciously limiting our hedonic activities could enrich our lives?

Art, like morality, consists in drawing the line somewhere.

—G.K. Chesterton

◆◆◆

I love coffee. Since my first cup at age 16 from Montana Coffee Traders' flagship roastery in Whitefish, I usually have two cups in the morning and another cup in the afternoon.

I will avoid debating the pros or cons of coffee consumption and only note that I love reading Scandinavian studies saying coffee is really good for us. Still, even a good-for-us thing can become a perceived requirement or an obsession.

In my twenties, I began to experiment with breaking habits—not necessarily bad habits, just habits I found myself overly attached to. If I sensed I was too dependent on something, I gave it up. For a year. One year in North Carolina it was TV. One year in Germany it was bras.

And one year in Oregon it was coffee.

No coffee for a full 365 days.

Three-hundred-and-sixty-five days.

Thank goodness it wasn't a leap year.

When the time expired, I celebrated with a cup of my estranged delight. Ever since that reuniting sip, I am grateful each and every time I lift my ceramic mug to my lips.[28]

Earlier, I mentioned hedonic adaptation. I could call this idea *lack adaptation,* but that doesn't exactly invite enthusiasm.

---

[28] Actually, the gratitude begins when I prep the coffee the night before, just *anticipating* that first cup in the morning. Anticipation again.

Maybe I won't try to call it anything. I won't even try to convince you to deprive yourself of anything intentionally. But I will say: it's deeply helpful if you want to live large on little.

When we give up one thing, we tend to look more closely at all the other things we take for granted.

More importantly, when we're grateful for all those things, we change our relationship toward them. Gratitude is the archenemy of taking things for granted.

Maybe I'll call it *gratitude adaptation.*

It's a funny thing about life, once you begin to take note of the things you are grateful for, you begin to lose sight of the things that you lack.

—Germany Kent

◆ ◆ ◆

When I taught on that very small island in Micronesia, the power usually went off at least once a day, if not more. Locals referred to the power company, the CUC, as "Customers Using Candles." The nights were usually so hot and humid that even a candle flame seemed to add to the heat.

The public high school where I taught English and art was built with cinderblocks, which was fine when the "aircon" worked. Not so fine when the power went off. If the deafening roar of the aircon wheezed to silence during second period, you were in for a long, hot day. By fourth period, it was hard to stand up straight, much less to think.

My fourth-period class was, if not so labeled, the remedial senior English class. They were mostly 17- and 18-year old boys, with a few older ones who had flunked the year before.

Not many people expected anything from these students, and they had learned to not expect much from anyone in return. They loved to play their ukuleles, and they kept the nails of their playing fingers long. Many of them were usually slightly stoned on betel nut—their magenta teeth a bright giveaway.

Maybe because of all that, their "aha" moments of learning are the ones I remember best.

Whenever one student in that class grasped the lesson—an implied metaphor or correct syntax—he would thump his desk with a smile, looking around at his friends, who would clap and call out sounds of approval similar to an audience at a poetry slam. Then, the one who just had his breakthrough would share it with his classmates.

Those students became some of my favorites.

For some reason, *Beowulf* was on the fall curriculum—a work of literature I had not encountered until college. And though most of my students spoke English as a second language, many in the remedial class could barely write it. So teaching an Old English text, even in translation, was a bit of an adventure. Thankfully, the action-packed tale is suited to teenage boys on the brink of manhood.

One of my favorite memories from those years of teaching was a day during the *Beowulf* unit. Fourth period had just started, and we had just opened the text books when the power went off.

I told the students to bring their books, and we left the classroom to tromp across the field to the shade of a lone flame tree, where enough breeze moved to keep the heat bearable. There, we all took turns reading aloud from the text.

I will never forget the cadmium red of the flame tree flowers who lived up to their name. The bluest tropical sky with an occasional cumulous cloud scuttling its puffy way toward the Marianas Trench. The lilting sound of my students' voices as they added dramatic flair and occasional reenactment to the ancient war scenes.

I learned many things from those students, including these three:

One: when you learn something, celebrate it. And then share it with others.

Two: sometimes, a limited power supply can invite us all into an unexpectedly blessed moment.

Three: never take electricity for granted.

In fact, on the rare occasion when the power goes out for one second and I have to reset my digital clock, I smile, offer up gratitude for the grace of the other 23.59 hours in the day it worked, and think of flame trees.

The Future Fruit

Keep some room in your heart for the unimaginable.

—Mary Oliver

◆ ◆ ◆

I spend my last day in San Francisco writing. At 3 PM, when the western side of Diamond Street is finally shaded, I start walking to the Ferry Building. My phone's GPS says it is 4.3 miles one way, but when I come home this evening, I will have walked ten miles.

As I get closer to the Embarcadero, I remember how busy this part of the city is, and I'm annoyed at having to break stride at every stop light.

My plan had been to treat myself to dinner—one of those Special Occasions—but when I arrive to the pier, my lower back is sore, thanks to an overactive day last summer of pickaxing a tree stump while landscaping. The pain sometimes kicks in when I go for long walks.

I am also hungry, but I don't want to eat the fruit leather I keep in my purse for moments of low blood sugar—which I probably should.

All to say: I am irritated.

To placate myself, I buy a sourdough cheese wheel, which is surprisingly awful, considering the bakery. The pastry is stale and hard. I take a few bites and am no longer hungry. I just want to be back in the studio where I can unroll the yoga mat and stretch, preferably with a glass of wine and a movie.

So I toss the remains of the cheese wheel and start walking all the way back.

As I trudge along Market Street, through the traffic lights and spindly urban trees, I wonder what this peninsula looked like before it was covered with concrete and skyscrapers.

Ahead, the elegant, flatiron Flood Building rises from the corner. When it was built over a century ago, it was the tallest building in the city. Now, it is dwarfed by gleaming towers.

I alternate between being annoyed at myself for overdoing landscaping last year and being annoyed at humanity for pushing itself to continual limits.

Then, at a red light, I stop—literally and figuratively. I am acting like a petulant toddler who needs a cookie and a nap.

As soon as I admit this, I laugh aloud at myself. I take advantage of the long stoplight to stretch my hamstrings. I say belated grace for the lousy pastry, noting that the expression "saying grace" is essentially the same as giving thanks—grace and gratitude are more linked than I thought.

I decide that instead of dinner, I'll buy a batch of expensive croissants before leaving the city in the morning and bring them back to my parents—which changes the dinner fail into an anticipatory delight.

When the light turns green, I look back up at the skyscrapers as I cross the intersection. "To push to the limits" is a kind of challenge, isn't it? Limitations really *are* invitations. To break the four-minute mile, to reach the moon, to do whatever we've been told is impossible.

That's where creativity comes in: finding the way to see the little—the restriction, the obstacle—as the portal to the large—the expansion, the gift. It's not always an easy choice or a smoothly continual one. Sometimes, creativity requires uprooting the old—like that tree stump last summer. Sometimes it requires a stubborn persistence to keep growing, like the trees of the Urban Forest Plan, determined to send their roots down and their branches up— even from within the confines of their small patches of concrete-encircled dirt.

Another red light. Another chance to stretch my legs and mind.

Logically, if I keep trying to live on less and less, I will eventually only succeed by living on nothing.

That is *not* my goal.

In fact, I'd be very, very happy with the opportunity to explore what it is to live large on large. But even if that never happens, I choose to be very, very happy[29] right here, right now—on a grimy city street corner. That's the heart of living large with whatever we have.

When the light turns green, I keep walking. I still have miles to go.

---

[29] As I said: I still confuse happiness with joy!

The best time to plant a tree was twenty years ago. The second best time is today.

—A Chinese Proverb

◆◆◆

In a way, our lives are one, big limitation-as-invitation, whatever our net worth. We have a finite number of days on this beautiful earth. What will we do with them?

One last imagination exercise before we go: a practice in future-self love....

Picture yourself twenty years from now. Where are you? What do you see and hear? Who or what are you surrounded by? What do you want to be feeling?

That feeling is part of your harvest—the result of years of gratitude given and grace received. The result of cultivating love, joy, peace, patience, kindness, goodness, faithfulness, and self-control.

What if we all planted good seeds, tended the fruit of our choices, and shared the bounty?

My feeling for the future?

The world would be much sweeter.

Gratitude unlocks the fullness of life. It turns what we have into enough, and more ....Gratitude makes sense of our past, brings peace for today, and creates a vision for tomorrow.

—Melody Beattie

Books by Anna Elkins

The Heart Takes Flight
The Honeylicker Angel
The Space Between
And: The Story of More

Books with Jan Elkins:

A Book of Blessings
Blessings for Love & War
Blessings of Hope & Joy
Blessings: A Children's Book for Grown-ups

Co-editor, with Christa Ammon:

Deep Travel: Souvenirs From the Inner Journey

Find out more at: **annaelkins.com**